Eternal Love

Eternal Love

A Poetic Pathway to God's Heart and Mind

C. Peggy Atoche

RESOURCE *Publications* · Eugene, Oregon

ETERNAL LOVE
A Poetic Pathway to God's Heart and Mind

Resource Publications
An Imprint of Wipf and Stock Publishers
199 W. 8th Ave., Suite 3
Eugene, OR 97401

www.wipfandstock.com

PAPERBACK ISBN: 978-1-6667-3615-1
HARDCOVER ISBN: 978-1-6667-9412-0
EBOOK ISBN: 978-1-6667-9413-7

DECEMBER 21, 2021 8:23 AM

To God and Jesus for your constant support, guidance, healing, love and efforts to help humanity grow into a more compassionate and loving state—Thank you. To my husband James (Jim), my mother Peggy (Maggie), Matthew and Tanya for constant support and love—Thank you.

To generations to come, may this be a helpful guide toward the Light and a way back home to God's love.

Contents

Introduction

*I*n a world highly affected by fear triggered by violence, social unrest, pandemics and natural disasters, finding light amidst darkness at times feels impossible. The goal of this book is to guide you through difficult times to a place of loving refuge and into a brighter future.

From the beginning of time, God has been a source of fear to some and of love to others. God has been labeled as a God of war who led armies into bloodbaths and yet He sent Jesus to this world to face cruelty without retaliating. We hear stories of "eye for eye, tooth for tooth" and yet Jesus taught us to turn the other cheek and forgive 70 times 7. Seems we have a lot of discerning and learning to do to understand the deep laws and principles embedded in God's messages.

"Discernment" and "Understanding" are two of many gifts God bestows upon those who fervently seek him.

Discernment helps us identify right from wrong, truth from falsehood; it helps us see clearly what is the best course of action to take in a given situation. Discernment helps us recognize, amidst the world's chaos, God's voice of truth and wisdom when He speaks to us.

The gift of understanding assists us during times of darkness and ignorance: when we don't seem to be able to choose right or left, forward or backward; when life brings us to a new crossroad and we are unsure of which way to take; when our conscience struggles with feelings of revenge after being hurt; when pain seems unbearable; when we have unanswered questions about life and death, good and evil; when we are confused by the vicissitudes of life. We might not be able to understand with our minds, but God has the power to imbue our hearts with a deep and clear understanding which guarantees us a path out of worry and apprehension into peace and acceptance. Understanding intuitively with our soul and heart, not relying solely on our logical mind, leads us to a more efficient and happier way to live life. This is especially true during tumultuous times.

The prose you'll find in this book is meant to guide you through the reading of the poems, to enhance your experience of the metaphors, messages and conversations, and to give you a little background to how the poems came to exist. You can choose not to read the text and challenge yourself to understand the poems without reading the explanations.

Finding peace and clarity is possible with God's guidance and help. My hope with this book of poetry is to draw a direct line from your heart to God's heart, which is filled with eternal love for you; to open a door and guide you to where He is and give you a chance to get to know Him as He truly is and not as what others say He is; to ask you to form your own opinion and make up your own mind about Him.

May His Voice, Light and Love guide you and keep you safe.

Looking at the Eyes of Jesus

This is one of my dearest poems. One evening I was admiring "The Prince of Peace," painted by Akiane Kramarik when she was 8 years old. Jesus' face looked so inviting. His gaze was warm and embracing, yet firm and strong. I was feeling exhausted, but I felt drawn to look intently at Jesus' eyes and as I did, I asked him to share with me some of his strength. I was being playful and never thought anything would come of it.

In a matter of seconds, it felt as if I had fallen off a cliff and into Jesus' eyes and into his world. I was not afraid, but I got very curious. The poem came right through me, and it took only a few minutes to write the verses down. What you read in the poem is what transpired at that moment.

I related my experience to my friend who is a theologist. She introduced me to "Gazing with icons," a practice that centuries ago was considered a form of prayer. Icons are images of holy figures created by those believed to have had a close connection with the divine. Believers gaze at these paintings and hope themselves to establish an intimate connection with the divine. I have come to think of this writing process as "Poetic Iconography."

I wrote this poem mid 2019 and a few months later I came across one of Akiane Kramarik's interviews. She said that one side of Jesus' face is covered with light and the other has a shadow over it. The shadow represents the suffering of this world. The tiny shaft of light emanating from the shrouded eye signifies that Jesus will always be with us when we go through trials or challenging times.[1]

This poem is a reminder to hold onto hope and faith. You are never alone.

---

1. Kramarik, "Lifeline Miracle Network 2005," 23:43.

Looking at the Eyes of Jesus

I am looking at the eyes of Jesus
looking for some of his strength
they look so deep, so vast, so still
I feel I am fainting
I am falling in . . .

Love is all through his being
irradiating light bursts through his eyes

one eye is filled with illumination
and in the other, a speck is all I find

within

this suffering that seems to be
part of his half-existential theme

I notice wrinkles on his forehead
to my surprise . . . mine are the same

Jesus' deep frown lines
furrowed in above his profound eyes
signify concern, love and hard work

A gentle-firm embrace
I suddenly feel as stillness
permeates my worn-out soul

"Stay still," he says in thoughts
"so I can share my peace, my love

No need to worry
life's not so hard
it only takes practice

to follow my commands"

"Good night, sweet Jesus"
I say, "goodnight
I am falling asleep"

A Father's Message of Love

*L*ate one morning, I was hoping to get inspired to write something about life, using the usual themes of storms and peace, life and death. This poem came through at the speed of light. At first, it was not clear to me what this poem was all about. It took me a while to realize that it was a direct message from our heavenly Father and took me much longer to understand the theme and intent. That morning, I prayed for inspiration to write a poem to send to a contest. But God had other plans, to deliver a poem to a different home—this poetry book.

Freedom can be seen from different perspectives—war is one of them. Freedom comes at a cost: war. When all diplomatic efforts have been exhausted during highly escalated conflicts in the world, war seems to be the only option to solve our problems. Pain, death, suffering, emotional and physical afflictions are consequences of war. The use of violence in the fight for freedom surpasses the moral limits of civilization and destroys respect for human life.

There is hope that one day, there will be no more tears.

A wonder that many aspire to and yet they cannot come to see the truth. The road to heaven is a steep one. We are not trying hard enough to understand the meaning of love and sacrifice.

Our spirits are made of love and we long to feel loved whether we are aware of this human need or not. We fail to experience love because our hearts are closed—we are afraid to love or feel loved. Sometimes, people act in ways that keep them away from experiencing true love (see "True Love Is Not Romantic").

Human life might not seem like a wonder, but it is a kind expression of life itself. Human life is only one expression among many. "Kind" because on this earth we have the opportunity to grow spiritually, to transform darkness into light.

Our world is at a young stage of spiritual growth, which means that wars, chaos, social unrest, emotional and spiritual disconnection among human beings are still part of our human experience. As we transform darkness into light and learn to understand the meaning of sacrifice, we slowly achieve spiritual growth and gain a higher level of compassion and awareness, and begin to truly love one another. Consequently, wars, chaos and disconnection start to decrease.

Can we truly achieve spiritual growth without God's help? Without a teacher and resources, can a student learn by him or herself? Can a person's strength alone be enough to remove a boulder from their shoulders?

The wonder of life brings still agonía (agony), in this stanza *Wonder* means puzzling. This word invites us to ponder about life, to be curious about the meaning of life.

The world is continually evolving, but there is still much work to do. God needs us to be *still* amidst the chaos, fear and uncertainty. When we are *still* we are more likely to accept God's strength, peace and love, and in turn, we can share these with the world. We can help raise the level of compassion and consciousness in people by making them aware of the suffering in this world.

We are free to choose (free will), but God is inviting us to come closer to his light.

A Father's Message of Love

Freedom comes with tears
and has no frontiers
bloodshed throughout the years
are nothing more than rebeldía.

Seems to me that a new day is coming
when no more tears are drained
from the heart full of love
that I gave once, in my Most

Funny thing is, love is always a mystery

Aquel feeling that runs in disbelief
A wonder that many aspire to
and yet they cannot come to see the truth

When this is all over
nothing will be left to doubt
All of the hurt, pain and misery
will be part of the past

Human life is but a wonder
a kind expression of life itself
Maybe to some it is all bonkers
but in the end it is all in your mind

My main reason for your existence
is that you learn to love again
I want nothing else than your progress
That is my final aim

There is no dubious intention in my being
for truth cannot be altered or misled
The purity of love is what we all seek
and in the end is hard to reach

Without my help, nothing can be done
for who can lift a rock that weighs a ton?
We all need many, to add strength
when we can't seem to bear the burdens of life

Finally, all's been said
The love, the life, the burden, the tears
The wonder of life brings still agonía
Much needs to be done — *Still* — in this world
I need your help to spread the love

Farewell, my darlings
I bid you well
Come closer to my light
and feel the fire of love inside

After a Battle, Mend My Heart

$\mathcal{A}$ time of reconciliation between God and humanity, a time for God to mend hearts. The battle of the heart refers to spiritual and emotional battles that may begin with disappointments in life, the ravages of war, losing a romantic partner, challenges with work or career, or anything that fits your definition of trouble.

Coming in tropel (throngs): this refers to all the horrors of war. PTSD, trauma, heartache, guilt and mental illnesses are experienced by many survivors. This poem describes the moment pain and madness become unbearable; the longing to find some help for those affected, to liberate them from these burdens, and quickly.

Humanity also comes in tropel to be fixed (healed) after natural disasters, pandemic and war. The healers or nurses represent God, Jesus, archangels or angels—all helpers in the spiritual realm.

Parting ways with sensatez (sanity) means losing soundness and clarity of mind. When we harm another, regardless of the reason, we try to justify the attack; God's divine law "do not kill" is violated. The use of violence to defend ourselves or others creates conflict within our conscience, which in turn, opens the door to mental illnesses. According to human reasoning, we defend ourselves with violence after all peaceful means have been exhausted. This does not make sense in God's spiritual realm.

God encourages us to use the power of collective prayer (many of us praying together) to transform violence into peace; God encourages us to respond to violence with prayers and seek the transformation of those who attempt to harm us. God is all powerful and has given us a very powerful tool: prayer. When we pray, we wish for an outcome; why not use prayer to bring healing, peace, unity and love into this world?

By connecting with God through individual and collective prayers, we can make manifest God's laws of peace on this earth.

Lord Oh Lord! is the moment we realize we have gone against our conscience and we desperately seek God for healing.

After a Battle, Mend My Heart

Love is in the air
Love is everywhere
I have heard this song
Before, once upon a time

A time for reconciliation
A time for mending hearts
The hearts of those in battle
The battle of the heart

Coming in tropel
After a trying week
Seek and find no one
Who can help them and be quick

The battles were too many
Sorrow, heartache, disbelief
They had to face the horror
That took their dignity

Who can mend a broken heart?
One that's seen so much
Bled to pieces while in sorrow
Parted ways with sensatez

Who can mend my broken heart?
Needs stitches miles long
Nurses running to the stretchers
War is over, Lord Oh Lord!

Take It Easy

Taking it easy is okay
Take it easy
And all is well

Open Your Heart

Open your heart my love
Open it without restraint
Open your heart to love
And blessings will rain

Love Song

I sing to love, I sing to God
For God is love, and I his song

I sing to peace, I sing to all
I sing to light, I sing to Might

His song is mine, and I am his
We melt together . . . Eternal Bliss

Cling to the Light

This poem refers to the importance of anchoring ourselves to our source of strength, love, peace—God's light. His light heals all wounds. Even in the harshest of times, even though we struggle to find God or to seek his love, remember to always cling to his light. In order to commence healing, we must be willing and ready or at least have the intention to start to heal, even if we don't believe it will happen. By clinging to God's light, we make slow progress, but progress nonetheless.

Cling to the Light

When danger lurks
Cling to the Light

When hope slips away
Cling to the Light

When sorrow comes
Cling to the Light

When life betrays you
Cling to the Light

When your heart is broken
Be healed by Light

When it seems confusing
Go ask the Light

When doubts and anger invade your soul
Cling to the Light

For God is love, and his Light heals
Never forget to cling onto Him

He is ready to cure all your wounds
Never let go

In the deepest of pain
Inside the darkest cave . . .

Cling to the Light, cling to the Light
with all of your might, with all your might

Nature and Love

*I*t is hard to find love in nature when images of wildlife documentaries come to mind. Predator eating prey: a rodent struggling to catch its last breath; blood and shredded skin splattered on the ground. This poem raises a thought-provoking question: when animals or humans harm others, is there love in them?

And yet, there is light radiating from everything we see in nature, from the tick to the Redwoods. The kind of light that can only be seen with our spiritual eyes.

Love is within and without; there is love inside all people and animals; and there is also darkness lurking.

Peace is unsettled, a lurker has arrived. Imagine a deer peacefully eating shrubs and a lion stalking nearby. This also represents our human condition: we are perpetrators and victims. When one animal eats another it satisfies its physical hunger. Similarly, human perpetrators commit crimes to feed the darkness within. Spiritual blindness strikes when wisdom, love, good sense and right mind are absent. When God's spirit within us is not strong enough, blindness occurs and with it comes the harming of others.

He is next down the line, refers to Karma or the laws of cause and effect. All action creates an equal reaction. All actions have consequences and what we do to others eventually comes back to us.

We are God's most beloved possession and as such when we hurt one another, our conscience comes into conflict. Our own judgment comes into play.

Nature and Love

I see Nature in Love
but do I see Love in Nature?

Love is within
and without

It exists
in doubt

Peace is unsettled
A lurker has arrived

to answer to its darkness
his appetite, blind . . .

to the wisdom of Spirit
who watches from nearby

The father of this Nature
sees with love nonetheless

The blind satisfies its blindness
but he is next down the line

to inflict on himself judgement
for harming Nature's Prize

Finding Paradise

I love you darlings
believe it or not. I am always around you
even when you choose not to see me

The song of paradise is at your fingertips
It seems slippery, missed by your grasp
Bend over, look for it . . . pick it up

May it guide you wisely
sweeten your day

Everything is alright, you see?
God's way is always best

The Purity of Love

G od seeks peace for this world. God is Love. No darkness can be thrown at God to change his love into evil.

" . . . the light in-sight," refers to the light that can only be seen with your spiritual eyes, which means the light you recognize with your heart and soul, the light you see in God.

As God's plan unfolds, it creates a ripple of peace, love and healing throughout the world. God's plan for this world is great; his vision can neither be seen with our physical eyes, nor heard by our ears, nor understood by our intellect.

God is part of us and he is ours to come to, talk to; in God we can seek healing and take refuge.

The Purity of Love

Peace is what I seek
Love is what I am
I am Love and I am yours
No love is greater than mine

No evil can cast shadows over Might
Sacred the energy within, powerful the light in-sight
Lovely, the size of my vision, it creates a lovely scene
A massive display of waves unseen

Love is what I am, don't ever hesitate
I am yours and you are mine
No one can doubt the essence of the Light
No one can taint with darkness the purity of Love

Love can't be doubted
Love is pure, strong and powerful
Love is love, love is strength
Love is Great

Surrender to the Light

We hear time and again of the importance of being in a state of peace and openness (humility) in order for God to channel his wisdom and love through us, so he can work on us, with us and for us. The greater the presence of God's light in us, the stronger and healthier we are.

Surrendering to the light means letting go of pride, arrogance and fear. It is difficult for God to work on us when these negative or low-vibration feelings block his light. Surrendering is never to be confused with giving up. Surrendering means letting go of burdens by letting God lighten our load.

It is easier for a patient heart to receive wisdom than a restless heart. Use the power of continuous prayer to get to a level of peace, stillness, openness and surrender.

Keep on praying and surrender; the ability to pray is a gift that has been given to all of us. Prayers can manifest as wishes, intense thoughts and longings. The more frequent and intense prayers are, the faster they will start to manifest. God is light and when our prayers align with him they align with principles of love, healing, unity and peace—this is another way to surrender.

We need to exercise awareness to make sure our prayers align with these principles and not with negative ones. Complaints, demands, criticisms, harmful requests, thoughts against others might seem like prayers, but they are not. God hears it all.

Surrender to the Light

Surrender to the Light
That which is divine

Asked for answers? got none?
Surrender with silence
And receive the Light

The wisdom of the ages
Comes right through
A patient heart

A restless mind
Blocks the peace of the Light

In order to get answers
Keep on praying and
Surrender to its Might

In the Light

*T*his poem touches on the spiritual phenomenon I experienced in 2012: "a dark night of the soul," also known as "spiritual awakening" or "spiritual rebirth." The goal here is to share the messages and wisdom I gained during this experience, such as how to reduce suffering in life and how to accept God's healing and love after many trials.

Resistance to painful experiences in life increases our suffering. Life brings pleasant experiences, but also challenging ones. While going through difficult situations, questions may arise, the most common one: why me? followed by thoughts that deny the experience: "it should not have happened to me." This initial phase of constant questioning is resistance: we can't seem to accept life as it is. The process of healing and recovery doesn't start until we begin to accept the pain and open our hearts and souls to healing. Unwillingness to forgive others is another way to resist the vicissitudes of life, and it also deters the process of healing—anger, resentment and feelings of revenge are harmful to ourselves as well as to others.

Accepting the reality of traumatic or painful experiences does not victimize us; on the contrary it empowers us. Acknowledging our experiences instead of hiding them, becoming aware of the pain instead of avoiding it—these practices strengthen our spirit and prepare us to accept God's healing and love and we start to grow spiritually. Healing is a process and it takes time to make progress. Be patient. At times circumstances might cause us to be deeply hurt and it might seem impossible to accept healing, but it is achievable.

In this poem, the cave represents the periods of darkness or pain we all go through in life.

Always aim higher, means no matter how broken you feel after a tragic experience, never settle for the cave and the shackles of victimization, anger and resentment. If you are biting dust, keep crawling. Staying in hellish states of mind such as anger, powerlessness, fear and revenge carries too high a price. Even if it takes years or decades to get up—get up.

Living in darkness under happiness's mirage, means to live on the surface, projecting a false sense of strength and "happiness" while burying unhealed pain in your heart. It also means, living with unresolved situations in life, such as not forgiving yourself or others; living with unhealed trauma.

Endure what comes your way; it isn't a loving being that wishes you pain. These verses are important as we often see ideas promoting God as a being who punishes, seeks revenge and condemns people to hell. He is Light and in Him there is no darkness at all.

One of God's teachings is the eternal practice of forgiveness. It is eternal because anger, pain or feelings of victimization have the natural tendency to return. We need to be on guard and keep our souls clean by the constant practice of forgiveness, and as we do this we become more like God.

Forgiveness is not to be confused with "lack of consequences." All acts of violence or harmful behavior carry a heavy weight; they weigh on our conscience and have consequences under spiritual law.

The other side, refers to darkness/evil in those who cause harm to others.

After all is finished, refers to a final phase: when we have achieved a state of forgiveness of ourselves and of others—we experience peace and joy.

In the Light

Today I am Light
It feels bright outside
Coming out of the deep cave
Is not for the faint of heart

I'm not saying I enjoyed it
I wouldn't choose it for myself
But we are guided by a greater
power . . . than ourselves

Not much gain in resisting
It causes more suffering
What helps is persistence
Follow the calling, finish your task

Life seemed unfair, we lost control
But we are guided by a greater cause
In the end the lessons learned help us all:
Our souls and those who still mourn

We can't fit much into our logic
We only understand when the deed is finished
Aim higher, always
And never settle for the dark

Inside the cave is temporary
It might seem eternal, but is not
The storm within seems to scar us
Well, it does

But some bruises are better
Than a life untouched
Still living in darkness
Under happiness's mirage

Truth hurts, so I heard
Well, it does
It heats up inside
We want to explode

Soothing the anger takes time
Healing is not as fast
As we thought it once
Endure what comes your way

It isn't a loving being that wishes you pain
The other side feeds upon it
But you are not them
And they know it

You are a being of love
That is why it hurts
Coming out of storms is not an easy task
But after all is *finished*, all will be fine

Responsibility and Love

When are activities in life a responsibility and when do we experience them as loving acts?

Sometimes, giving to or serving others might seem a responsibility, services performed with a sense of obligation instead of appreciation.

The scope of responsibility covers charitable work, parenting, caregiving, leadership, writing, singing, painting, preaching, any activity that we engage in to provide others with our time and skills.

The message in this poem resonates with my experience of responsibility and love. The gift of writing came to me unexpectedly and changed my life radically, throwing me into a period of great suffering. I had not gone to school to learn this skill, which made writing a foreign concept to me. I resisted taking on the weight of responsibility of developing this new craft—and this resistance added to the pain. As I started to respond positively to this calling, the burden started to wear off. It took me years to go from experiencing struggle and pain to a state of acceptance and love.

When we reach a level of love for others, as God loves us, we no longer see our work as responsibility but as a privilege, and in time, we learn to honor our roles in life.

Responsibility and Love

It is responsibility to a human mind
But an act of love from God's mind

And what is an act of love?
is it kisses and hugs?
loving gazes and more?

Love is
to give, to serve, to bring
out the innermost
from your soul

What is an act of love?
to write your melody
to organize your words
to make them rhyme
to make them clear
to soothe the wounds
of souls in fear

What is an act of love?
it is not a duty
not a must
it is wanting, longing
it is freedom, at last

It is no burden to love
it is a privilege
for when love is not present
responsibility shows up

With responsibility
comes the fears
the worries
the stress
the cold nights

With love, duty becomes leisure
every task is an immense delight
Let's throw the sense of duty out the window
and bring the warmest love inside

In Love I Pray

In Love I pray
For Love I pray
With Love I pray

I pray . . .

I pray for All
May All pray for me
May We pray for each other

We Pray . . .

Pray for the World

It's time to pray, it's time to sing
Pray for us all, pray for them
Pray for the world, pray for yourself

Send blessings everywhere!

The healing word of God has been slain
By those who hear, but cannot read
The message hidden, the truth revealed

Pray for them

The loved, the hated
The cursed, the blessed
The healed, the hurt
The chaos, the rest

Pray for the world

Servant is not low but high
In human estimation, servant is low
But is high to the one above

Send blessings everywhere

The highest and most honored
Glorify the father
Shower blessings, light and wisdom
Upon souls below who lack reason

Pray for us all

Awakening to Your Purpose

"*A*wakening to your purpose" is a narrative whereby I am guided through a period of darkness and out into the light.

This poem unfolds an exchange with God that many of us have already experienced while facing challenging times. The verses describe aspects of a spiritual awakening and rebirth. The messages found in this poem are intended to motivate you to keep moving forward through difficulties and to find and accept your calling in life.

God encourages us to help ourselves, to heal and become strong; then we can use our experience of difficulty to guide others and help them find strength, joy and peace. This poem reminds us that love, like glue, has the power to bind all our pieces together after we have been crushed and scattered by life's experiences. When you have reached your lowest point in life, and feel that you have no more to give to yourself or others, remember that love has incredible healing powers and can strengthen you again.

God's hope for each of us is that we may brighten someone else's spirit, uplift those who, like us, have been deeply affected by difficulties, and show them the way back "home" to an inner place of peace, strength and connection with God—our source of love, light and strength.

Awakening to Your Purpose

Everything turns dark
a massive invisible hand
presses my body down
a force shoves my soul into stillness

I leave the busyness of living
and begin a silent life

Time goes by, then God speaks:
There is something you must do
Please help the weak of spirit
for they have no strength to move

I myself am in weakness
Can't you see my soul was crushed?
You ask the dead for miracles
How am I to be the light?

Now you are blind, but wait and see
Only time will cure your sight
Love will glue together the broken rays
and restore your light

Your sight will come back to health
The light inside will grow brighter than before
to radiate love to those in disgrace
who don't seem to be moving or have life at all

It is important to help those who are weak
You are strong and have much to give
You asked for this once in the past
before your birth, while among the stars

Now, go out and reach your destiny
which you promised, once upon a Light
and bring me news of your success:
that what was faint light is now more intense

Rewards are for the brave
for those who choose to risk their life
for they know the courage within them
will be enough to increase the light

No one dies for trying, souls never die
I give you the gift of eternity, you give me the gift of life
I love you little ones
believe it or not, with all my heart

Come back in victory
I need your brothers by my side
I miss them as much as I miss you
Come back to me multiplied

Go write, sing, co-create
My hands are tied if you defer
We are One and without you
life gets dimmer instead of turning bright

Goodbye for now, I am waiting
for news to come from afar
of your great success while weathering
the cold side of the light

Love Is Love

*H*ow do we define love?

God's love for us is blind: he sees no color, no shape, no level of wrong. His love extends to those who have committed harm against others. God sees potential for growth in those who have little love in their spirit; he sees them with compassion. This compassionate approach aligns with Jesus' principle of loving those who harm us and praying for them. God's love is eternal for all, with no exceptions.

Regardless of cruelty and how we treat God (such as when Jesus was crucified), God continues to assist human beings to grow and evolve spiritually.

War, crime, famine, social disconnection—all require God to keep on parenting humanity. He invites us to align with principles of love and peace. This task seems eternal, but in reality time never ends. The *ticking* represents humanity's transition into a new era. This transition also represents humanity's spiritual growth (evolution).

Hurrying God won't help. Physical, emotional and spiritual healing take time. Stay still and invite the healer do his job.

Meditation and prayer are practices that help us become still. When we are in a state of stillness, with open and humble hearts, God can share his love with us and teach us principles to help our spirits evolve so we may experience higher levels of compassion toward ourselves and others.

Love Is Love

Love is Love
Love, is Love
Love is, Love

An age-old question:
What is Love?

Love is blind, so I hear
Like my love, love does not disappear

No matter how cruelly I am treated
I keep coming back, to unending bliss

To give up, not likely
I see the challenge, and I take the Lead

For parentless children
Love is a sight to see

My guidance? or your way?
Both align until the end

The end of time
But does it end?

Or keep on going?
It's just the ticking that seems to change

Keep my pace
Difficult task

Hurry up!
Won't help much

Stay Still
That will do!

Only Patience
Will cure your wounds

Love is Patience
Patience in Love
Love is Love
Love, is Love.

Long-Lost Love

*A*ny loss in life is difficult and at times can feel unbearable. When our loved ones part from us, transition to the spirit world, or when we mistakenly feel the absence of God's love, we experience the pain of loss and separation—this is a mirage, not real, for we are eternally connected to one another and to God in spirit.

We can never lose someone we have loved, even those who have surpassed the limits of time and dimension. God creates each soul to be interconnected. We are never separate, not even after death. The belief that we lose people when they die is an illusion because our souls are eternal. Only the physical body departs; love always remains with us. It is the excessive fear of losing someone or having lost someone that creates a painful emotional attachment to the idea of "loss" that at times can become a burden to carry—this fear is a lie.

After a period of suffering, and when we are ready, we can begin to free ourselves from this burden by not feeding the idea of loss and instead free up space in our hearts for feelings of acceptance, understanding and peace. We are never separate or disconnected from our loved ones because love surpasses time and dimension. What does this mean? That physical life (as human beings in physical bodies) is one dimension, and the spiritual world is another. Once our lives end in this world, our spirits cross over to the spiritual realm and we bring our love with us into eternity.

In either realm or dimension, love is always part of our spiritual existence. The spirits of our loved ones are filled with warm light and love which always lives in our hearts when we choose to believe. God's love is eternal and we are never separate from him. When we choose to believe in God and fervently seek him, we'll find Him.

Long-Lost Love

My soul weeps
for a love far beyond
the understanding of time

God whispers to my heart:

A caress of my hands
will wipe off your sadness
but if you resist, the pain will linger a while
It is not "truth" you feel

The mirage of loss is what you fear
but we never lose one another
we are forever connected in Love
it is only time that keep us apart
but with each passing moment, understand
that we are all connected, that Love is always here
it never leaves . . .

it is all good, it is now time to learn
to detach from that which does not serve
your eternal need to be free
do not carry the burden of lies
the mirage of attachment is "one more lie"

Freedom lies in letting go
of that which does not serve the truth of Love
Love is eternal, and so are we
all in this together, on this earth
we never separate, we only say, see you later
I will be seeing you soon, and soon will come . . .
another soon, part of eternity, you see?
there never is a final goodbye

Sadness

Sadness comes
sadness goes
sadness never
stays long . . .

I love you

True Love Is Not Romantic

True love as defined by spiritual law means to love all, not just one person or group of people. God's love is true love. God's love seeks the welfare of all, not just of some. True love can see beyond appearance, color and creed, beyond mental and physical ability or disfunction.

True love can see possibilities in the darkness, the potential of lost souls to be transformed. Our society tends to define true love as romantic love. True love seeks the welfare of all, not just two. True love means to be of service to others; to reach as many people in need as we can; to not differentiate amongst ourselves—to treat all others equally. God's love is true.

True Love Is Not Romantic

True Love is not romantic
is loving without agenda
without ulterior motive
without self-seeking

True Love seeks the welfare of others
the wellbeing of others

True Love is not romantic
is expansive

It embraces the masses
like a bear hug
cuddly yet strong

True Love is seeing the unseeable
the diamond in the coal
the brightness in the dark
the warmest in the cold

True Love is not comparing
what we need with what they have

Though there is Love in romance
romance isn't True Love
Romance thinks of two, a limited view
Love thinks of All, a much broader view

True Love is not romantic
it reaches us all
Romance serves only two
True Love serves all

Forgiving Is Hard, Not Impossible

*H*ow can we stop violence in the world?

This is a question we have been asking for thousands of years. God's wisdom unfolds throughout this poem and points to an answer.

We are encouraged by spiritual laws not to judge but to forgive others, regardless of the violence perpetrated against us or others. Easier said than done—most victims of violence will not be quick to forgive and will not live by this law. Nevertheless, the only way to stop violence permanently in this world is through the practice of forgiveness. Forgiveness is not likely to occur immediately after a tragic event, unless those suffering are spiritually evolved—as Jesus was when he forgave his aggressors from the cross as he was brutally killed.

Forgiveness is a process and as such requires time. It also requires the willingness to commence healing on both sides: by perpetrators and victims. Prayer is a powerful tool. Forgiving and praying for the transformation of the perpetrators, enable victims to move from a state of victimization to one of empowerment.

At times forgiving is seen as a sign of weakness, but it requires character to forgive. Jesus dying on the cross showed strength and also taught us forgiveness and love can neutralize evil. His powerful message to forgive those who tortured and eventually killed him, teaches us how to stop the endless circle of violence in our world. Jesus never lifted a finger to counteract violence, no matter how powerful and able he was. Forgiveness does not exempt perpetrators from experiencing consequences for their actions in the spiritual and physical world.

Darkness (evil) cannot survive where prayers live—prayers are light. When we send prayers to those who cause harm, we transform their hate and their need to inflict pain on others into love; we indirectly imbue their conscience with a desire for contrition, transformation and healing. By condemning and punishing we keep these souls in a permanent hell and once there, they release energy back to us in the way of violence—there is no growth, therefore, and violence perpetuates. Prayers help souls return to

God's light and learn to exist by the principles of love. God is the master of transformation; when prayers reach him, he commences the work.

In this poem "the link that evil forms" refers to the invisible spiritual link established between aggressor and victim. The goal of this link is to transfer the darkness of pain, anger, and more violence to the victim, and feed it permanently—this is how negative energy (evil) survives. Prayers break this link. The darkness of violence within the hearts of those who harm cannot survive prayers and acts of love and forgiveness directed toward them. Once forgiveness has been applied, it must be maintained as the hurt tends to come back and the link attempts to re-establish itself. Prayers and forgiveness strengthen your soul; this is where your true power lies.

Forgiveness can be seen as impossible, but it is truly achievable. Please contemplate giving your time, effort and willingness to truly wanting to step out of the circle of violence in order to end it—we can all contribute to peace in this world.

Forgiving Is Hard, Not Impossible

Sadness, shock and pain
on a dark and gruesome day
a man committed a crime—
a lost soul, out of his mind

A soul battling darkness
a soul in distress
a soul could not speak
while evil acted out of hate

Why does this happen?
tragedy after tragedy
time and again
it happens every day

Forgiveness?
I think not
start with softness?
apparently not

Only time dictates
the song that flows
out of our hearts
if we dare to explore

Sooner or later
we must learn to forgive
for evil cannot survive
where love dares to live

Tolerance and prayers
transform the darkness
that lurks outside the hearts
of people who've lost those they love

The link that evil forms
when acting out its deed
is still attached
to those who don't forgive

Believe it or not
forgiveness is the tool you need
to sever the link
that enemies create to harden your heart

For love hurts them through forgiveness
and hurt is what they won't take
it is easy for them to impose pain
but it is a thing they cannot sustain

Free yourself from the ties of darkness
it seized your soul when you were unguarded
it has your hate, your anger, your pain
all that ignorance is its daily bread

Send it love, transform the evil
turn it back into the bright star
it was once upon a time
when things were created

filled with light
when even darkness
once
was light

Love Is Indestructible

*T*he kingdom of love is eternal and God will always reign. Nothing can detain God's love and stop his power. Not even "free" will.

"The lifeline of our existence" refers to both physical and spiritual existence. The physical body needs air to breathe to live. The spirit uses love as its air to survive.

It is unnatural and impossible to destroy the energy of love. Free will has a natural tendency to go against love. Our own light and conscience will never perpetuate anything that goes against us. The crooked trajectory of *free will*, in time, will eventually align with God's principle of love. Love always wins.

Love Is Indestructible

Love will always reign
always win
nothing can detain its power
nor match its force

Not even sheer *will*

Love is limitless
Love is boundless
Love is ever giving
Love is sacrificing

Nothing beats the power of Love
No one can defeat that which is
unending, untouchable, un-tarnishable

Destroying Love is like destroying air
which seems light, weak, invisible, non-existent
yet holds the power of Life itself
the lifeline of our *existence*

Some want to use swords to destroy air
But can they?
Some want to use guns to destroy air
But can they?
Some want to use magic to destroy the *unseen*,
But can they?

So, love—indestructible like air
unseen, unheard, untouched, only felt by our hearts—
can never be destroyed by swords, guns, or magic

The power lies in its essence:

Love is stillness
Love is peace
Love is eternal
Love is fierce
Love is unbending
Love is relentless
Love is unending

So, you "see"?
many will "try" to destroy what scares them
they fear Love

But their quest will someday cease
their "will" will be transformed
and in the end
one day they too
will abide in Love

Love is King
Love always wins

Eternal Love

$\mathcal{M}$y gift of writing was born out of a deep, transformative spiritual experience I went through many years ago. After writing in different genres for the first few years after that "moment of awakening," my first poem came through unexpectedly one afternoon. I had just woken from a nap and was in a semi-conscious state, between the realm of dreams and waking reality. God and I were having a conversation—and I was in tears, literally.

The exchange of thoughts ("the conversation") between God's consciousness and mine took place in an instant, rather than back and forth in "linear time"; this was not a real-life conversation where people take turns speaking, listening, responding. God's thoughts and mine overlapped, I felt the urge to write down our unspoken conversation quickly before the words slipped my mind. When I finished, I realized the dialogue took the shape of a rhyming poem.

This poem captures most of the "consciousness exchange" that took place between God and me that afternoon. Words in three different languages easily flowed into this poem: English, Spanish (te amo, vaivén, besos, prosa), and one word in Swedish (Pappa). My first poem was trilingual.

With this poem I hope to convey as much love as I felt while in God's spiritual bosom that day, which is the same love he feels for each one of us. One of the many ways God expresses his love for us is by singing "I love you" non-stop in infinity. Even though at times we might not hear or want to acknowledge his love, his love for us is present and eternal.

"Outside it is so dark" refers to a state of existential depression. During such times, no matter how sunny it is outside, everything looks bleak, and dark.

"Why not lend a helping hand / to those on their knees / who have not yet learned to stand" poses a question for self-reflection to those healthy and strong enough to help but who do not help others struggling in life.

"Why suffer when you can love? . . . " This question invites us to trust and have faith that all difficult experiences end and nothing is permanent; we are invited to trust instead the process of life. The stanza also encourages us to reflect on the pain we create when we are not fulfilling our life's purpose. Resisting difficult changes in our life's circumstances creates unnecessary suffering and blocks our capacity to love. Aligning ourselves with God's spiritual laws and becoming aware of his purpose and plans brings a sense of ease and peace into our lives.

"Drowning in despair" in the following stanza symbolizes the state we are in when going through the storms of life. When we experience losses or painful changes in life, we are tempted to doubt God and his love. Pain can be blinding. Meanwhile, in the depths of our hearts, we know who God is, and by tapping into this knowledge, no matter how faint or weak we feel, we remember that God is love and only the chaos of our present circumstances is distorting this truth. Let your hand reach for God and trust that he can be the help you are looking for in the worst of times.

The last stanza of the poem refers to the peace we find when we align with our life's purpose and with God's principles. The words of the last stanza also reflect the final resting place our spirits go to when we transition from the physical world to the spiritual one.

Eternal Love

My love for you is eternal,
God's devoted voice resounded.
"My love for you is eternal,"
my own voice chimed.

"I love you, I love you, I love you,"
together we sang ∞
"Te amo Pappa, God,
a thousand times over,

and I am sorry,
I am tired,
I want to cross over—
to a place of peace
and eternal bliss."

Perhaps not tomorrow,
perhaps not today—
if my soul can take the sorrow,
at your will, it'll happen any day.

I hope my love is true,
not born of a place of fear;
I hope this arduous road ends soon
for all I have now are continued tears.

Outside it is so dark—
When is the sun coming out?
Will it rise tomorrow?

Bystanders keep idle watch
while the meek stumble and perish.
Why not lend a helping hand
to those on their knees
who have not yet learned to stand?"

God tenderly quelled my doubt:

Why suffer when you can love?
Why cry when you can laugh?
Why create endless pain?
All you need is to trust and have faith.

My heart was wide open
as God and I shared this moment,
and memories of an earlier time's
dark night came to mind:

"It was confusing to get to know you
in this world of vaivén:
how to make you out while inner tumult and mess/
blinded me and was hard to escape.

As I was drowning in despair
I felt your hand outstretched, to me,
and as I reached to seek salvation,
you wrapped me in your love and cozy besos.

Now I can rest, my breath at peace;
now I can feel the ocean's breeze;
now I can search for that fine bliss
I mentioned earlier in prosa—"

Twin Poems

O ne day, God presented me with a vision. I saw myself surrounded by divine light, and the word "beauty" was written upon this image.

Two poems came. As I finished writing the second, I realized that both poems shared the same message and rhyme scheme, and the final stanzas carried similar words and meaning.

To dress in beauty means to be clothed in God's light, love, peace, wisdom and healing energy. Within these verses, you will find a hidden call to use the powerful tool of collective prayer in order to help our world heal.

When we feel our own spirit light up while surrounded by God's light, we are encouraged to pray fervently for our world. Abundantly means to pray frequently and to expand our daily prayers to take in the entire globe.

Together refers to people praying collectively. I wrote these poems in 2018 before the 2020 outcry for racial equality, and the climate change devastation caused by natural disasters such as the wildfires in Australia and North America and the Amazon during 2019–2020. News articles across the globe marveled at the power of collective prayer at these critical times. Some examples are: the sudden change in wind direction that saved lives from the fires in the town of Mallacoota, Australia;[2] the heavy rainfall that dampened Australian forest fires after Muslims and Christians prayed together in the town of Adelaide and the collective prayers offered in Glastonbury Tor, UK;[3] the miracle of policemen on their knees praying together alongside protesters all over the US after the murder of George Floyd in Minneapolis.[4]

Never walk alone means never go without God's joy, wisdom, or his peaceful and protective light.

Walk in beauty means to walk with Jesus' light, to be filled with prayers from his heart. The beauty of the ages means the wisdom of experience

---

2. Abbott, "Prayer Saved Thousands in Mallacoota."
3. "Australian Muslims"; Gladwin, "Rain Brings Relief"; "Australia Fires: Heavy Rain."
4. O'Kane, "Police Officers Kneel."

throughout eternity. Jesus' light embodies the gifts of unity, wisdom, love, healing, joy, peace and hope.

Twin Poems

i. I dress in beauty

I dress in beauty, I walk in love
healing surrounds me, love is on

I dress in beauty, sparkling light
radiating from every part of my soul

My prayers emanate abundantly
and expand to all corners of the Earth
transforming the world's turmoil into peace

It is my wish, my song:
together and always . . . walk in love
always dress in beauty
. . . never walk alone.

ii. I walk in beauty

I walk in beauty
covered in light
filled with prayers
from thy heart

I walk alone . . . never
in love . . . forever
I walk and don't look back
in splendor . . . majestic sight

I walk with friends . . . a must
walk with teachers . . . so wise
I walk in darkness . . . jamás
walk and don't run . . . God's best advice

The beauty of the ages
walks with me
Love surrounds me
dwells within

I walk in beauty, always
that is my wish
always walk in beauty
. . . never walk alone

Poverty and Love

*T*his poem unfolds concepts of spiritual and material poverty.

I have met people who are kind to others in distress and I have also come across those who mock, judge and haughtily show off their ability to cope with life to those who are struggling, saying, "If I can do it, so can they; they are a disgrace to society," or, "They are lazy. I work hard, why can't they?" or "It is all about willpower, don't give excuses."

Their criticisms and judgements target the homeless, those on social assistance, those affected by addiction or trying to overcome addiction, and those who have been so shocked by tragic events or violent life changes they are not able to get back into the swing of life.

Words and actions are unseen weapons that can cause emotional and spiritual damage. Under spiritual laws, there are serious and painful consequences for those who judge and put others down.

The horizon is the kingdom of heaven where people are clothed in the light of love. A place of peace and joy.

Our level of strength determines how our spirits will respond to challenging times. Under extreme circumstances, where basic necessities such as food, shelter, safety and protection are lacking, emotional health is affected; this results in a lack of self-esteem, confidence and appreciation. In this state, people often show little or no hope for the future. The human spirit can sink very low—to a place where there is no strength to stand up or even to continue living. This poem is a calling to not judge or ignore people who are down in life and in need of help.

They dress in beauty means to be covered by God's light, the richest possession we can have.

Poverty of the soul here means to be low in spirits. This does not mean lack of wisdom or conscience.

Above the wide horizon implies a life of frivolous existence. It is wide because it is filled with egotism, a sense of superiority, a lack of satisfaction for life and an unending craving for more tangible possessions and excessive pleasure.

We hear time and again "the road to heaven (home) is long, narrow and steep," not an easy hike. A much longer road awaits those who look down on others who lack strength or health.

To give implies not only to offer financial help, but also to offer time, knowledge, love and words. These gifts can uplift any human being, rich or poor, who is down in spirits, who needs to connect to other souls, who needs to be loved. Our kind and wise words, love and encouragement carry the power to set free those who believe they are cursed and cannot progress in life.

It is worth clarifying that there are wealthy people with compassionate and giving hearts. This poem does not mean to glorify material poverty or vilify wealth. God knows our physical and material needs, and finding a healthy balance leads to joy, love, peace and a clean conscience. God encourages us to be responsible with money, power and fame, to use these tools responsibly and always in service of others.

Poverty and Love

Poor, bound and shackled
they can't seem to progress
their freedom is withheld

The horizon is not visible
seems too far away
they walk along life's path
but can't seem to see the end

Rags are all we see, pity is what we feel
but this is nothing more than a mirage
an invaluable jewel is hidden inside
the treasure is in their hearts

Without clothes, objects and belongings
they dress in beauty covered in gold
the brightest shiniest light they hold
they walk in grace and so much more

There is poverty of the soul
hopeless and in the dark, they wander in limbo
have no strength to stand up
they wait for help
hope soon arrives

But right above *the wide horizon*
where lies the kingdom of the wealthy
are riches, lust and vanity aplenty

A long way home
awaits the ones
who look down
on those whose hope is lost

Love is kind, Love is rich

Love is free, Love is "to give"

Love awaits those who travel
the steep journey of the *Giving*

They free the ones who cannot walk,
bound by chains of loss
They break the chains, give them keys
to unlock their curse and set them free

A Moment With God

God came to talk to me
One afternoon when I longed for him

For answers, explanation, a course to take
An explanation of why

I felt sad, afraid and frustrated
Ashamed, angry and exposed

At last He came and asked me in thoughts
In a vision, his hand holding a pen

To write down some notes
I thought at first I'd imagined the whole thing

But then my pencil followed the ideas
I started to write God's thoughts about me

His feelings and advice so I could be calm
I wrote and wrote 3 long pages

It didn't seem to be my mind
A message seemed to be written

From a father to his daughter's heart
So she could relax

Turn it over to him
And give him the burden

I felt lighter

Jesus' Vision for the World

Jesus' vision for the world
is much more than eyes can behold
in your heart you know this is true
filled with Love, his heart is yours

Jesus knows our every move
right or left, he knows what's best
when we lean on him, we learn to listen
and all his wisdom we can access

Jesus' vision for this world
is bigger than what eyes behold
look deeper and you will find
that his mirada is an homage
to God's Spirit, our heavenly father

Our Lord and Saviour is our salvation

Look further and you will find
a world of peace behind His face
a world of Love, hope and rest
not found here, in this world of mess

Jesus' vision for this world
is a massive load of Love
sweat and tears—tons of work
It is ambitious

Jesus wants to reunite
souls that drifted apart
when darkness condemned them

He will reconnect our souls
with love and peace
He aims to restore the *harmony*
once established *in the beginning.*

Jesus: *My vision for this world is filled with love, hope and more*
is greater than human eye can see
stretches beyond what human mind can imagine
outstretches the outskirts of space

My vision for this world is unique
no man can fathom it, guess it
Can you imagine the wildest dream
put into words and make it happen?
Can you imagine the wildest dream
put in thoughts and then in action?

My vision for this world is never ending
it seems far-fetched
but is reachable
in fact, reachable

With the help of many

His burden becomes lighter
it becomes lighter . . .

A Father's Love

*G*od's love for us is shown by the sacrifice Jesus made in order to leave with us the gifts of love, compassion, forgiveness, peace, equality, fairness, and wisdom, among others. Jesus also left a set of rules to live by in order to achieve spiritual growth so we could grow closer to God's spirit. The trials of life continue to this day. Jesus came to show us how to love more and how to end our own suffering and that of others: by abiding in God's teachings and welcoming his love.

That I carried out my greatest job refers to the excruciating suffering Jesus endured during crucifixion in order to leave us an enduring legacy. God's love is sacrificial: as Jesus suffered, so did God. As we suffer, so does God.

Jesus came to teach us to love one another so we could grow spiritually. When we learn to love, our compassion increases and as it does so does our spiritual strength—we grow spiritually. To accomplish this, we need God's guidance and wisdom, very much like plants need nutrients, light and water to live and to grow. When our love increases, we are closer to God's spirit—our spiritual home.

God awaits our return home, to hold us close to his bosom. This is a place of peace, love, strength and stillness. When we align with God and allow His light to enter our hearts and minds, we align with heaven. Heaven is not only a physical place we aspire to go to after we die, it is also inside us. When we partner with God's spirit and love, we are home, we are in heaven. Heaven is a place we can all take refuge in while the turmoil and chaos of this world continues to unfold.

A Father's Love

A Father's Love is infinite
A Father's Love is transcendent
His Love is unique
He is Love itself

His Love can move mountains
Create rains
Showers of Grace
And Winds of Faith

My Love for you is infinite
Is sacrificial
Is all I have to give
Take it, don't take it
My Love for you is Choice
My gift, my token of appreciation
Just for being You

My Love for you is blind
My Love is wide and endless
Come to me child
Father is waiting for you
Under His wings you'll be safe
Filled with Love
That only in His heaven will you find

Come to me children
Love me as I Love you
For my Love is eternal
It never runs out
It is patient and Light
Clear and wide

My Love for you is so great
That I carried out my greatest job
Come to me children, come to me
Father is waiting . . .

Always . . .

We use the word "always" to define our life's circumstances: we will always be joyful; we will always be safe; or we use "never": we will never recover from this illness—we create our own joy and suffering. But nothing stays in a permanent state—life changes constantly.

Uncomfortable and harmful feelings such as hate, envy and anger will eventually change. "I'll always hate that person"—that seems permanent, but sooner or later in this life or after it, our spirits will learn to forgive. All unhealthy feelings will eventually transform.

Life chooses what and where it will go. When circumstances change so does our "always." When life changes, in positive or negative ways, so does the situation we thought would last. Life changes include the death of a loved one, a new job, a disability, the healing of what seemed an incurable illness.

We have a natural tendency to love those we get along with, and keep at arm's length those we dislike or who hurt us. But we need to learn to love those we consider our enemies; we need to learn to love people we believe deserve to be judged, criticized and ostracized; we need to practice forgiveness in order to create healing in everyone as well as in ourselves.

"You can't love someone or something always / because nothing and no one last forever"—so reduce suffering by not excessively attaching to the identities of friends, children, spouses, etc. Find a balance between loving others and always loving God first; this reduces suffering because God is the only one who stays permanently with us; we can never lose him; He never dies.

Someday all the people we meet on this earth will return to God. Our identities are temporary, but our spirit, which does not have a name, is eternal. In spirit form, in heaven, we have no name; we are all equal and the same. So we can love our spiritual state eternally, but not the temporary identities we are given while we live on earth. We always return to God and in his spirit we always and eternally live as He is the only eternal being.

Always . . .

No need to add anything to *Always*
Let it be . . .

For if you add anything
You condition Life to do your will

Always doesn't let you choose
It is already chosen for you

Always is to Love
But is not who to always love

Love "all" always
But don't precondition who to choose

You can't love someone or something *always*
Because nothing and no one lasts forever

But you can choose to always love them
In a way that doesn't confine your love to this life

Always implies eternity
Yet we leave this life some day

Our identity in this lifetime
Will end someday

But our spirits live forever
So we can love each other forever

Always goes hand in hand with eternity
So don't place always before a temporary

Feeling, idea, person, thing
Or circumstance

Let it be
The only thing for sure that

Will always be
Is God's spirit

Eternally existing in
Oceans of love

Life Never Ends

When loved ones depart and transition to the spiritual world, their absence might feel like a loss, but in reality we never lose anybody. We never truly die, our spirits live eternally. When we open our hearts to feel our loved ones' spiritual light, warmth and love, we find that they are always present with us in spirit, and in the legacy they have left behind.

This understanding can also be applied to the physical separation we experience during relationship breakups or relationship hardships of any kind, such as children separating from their parents, close friends moving away, marital separation or divorce.

Whichever circumstance you might be going through, it is important to remember that when people are no longer physically present, their love remains in spirit. If those you have loved have caused harm in any way, you can hold onto the love they gave you, but if this is not possible, remember that God's eternal love and presence is always available to you. He is ready and willing to embrace you and help you heal. When you call for and invite him into your life, you will find his love. It is always with you and inside you. He is the greatest spiritual companion and healer you could ask for.

Life Never Ends

You cry in silence
Smile out loud
When someone parts ways
With your grieving soul

Hope is not lost, it is not the end
For we always return
To that land of magic
Far beyond this world

Wandering in our minds, lost
We grieve the spirit that once was close
Grieve and nurse our wounds
Under a large and perfect moon

The friendship, love and memories
Seem far gone, so hard to hold
Sooner or later the pain will go
But the love inside us stays strong

Goodbye is only temporary
We will reunite soon
Time heals the mirage of loss
All that matters is the legacy of love

Love Always Wins

And so it does . . .

Nothing challenges this truth
For truth cannot be challenged
If it tries, it will soon fail

Truth is truth
There is no half truth

Can the sun be halved?
Or the moon?

Their state can be altered by perception
But not their true form

Nothing can touch them
Except our minds

And in minds
Distortions happen

Perceptions alter colors
Change shapes, misinterpret meanings

But in reality
The sun and the moon stay the same

Strong, bright and seen

At times, they change
But only in your mind

Let it Be

Don't force anything in Life
When it comes, it comes

Don't force anyone into your life
When they come, they come

Don't force time on anyone
When it is time, they'll come

When it's time, it's time
When the time is right, it is right

Patience is your strongest ally
Partner with it well

So it might help you
Get through challenging times

And come out to the other side
Successfully—in peace

I love you

Jesus Is Praying for Me Tonight

The main theme in this poem is unconsciousness. When our mind and spirit drift away, we fall into unconsciousness. Spiritually unconscious means to be disconnected from spirit—the force God placed inside us which is governed by conscience and filled with strength, courage, awareness, love, wisdom, peace and stillness.

When we are spiritually unconscious we fall into self-destructive behaviors, such as overindulgence, addiction, escapism, depression and uncontrollable anger. We might use words unwisely, causing harm to ourselves and others. We might feed toxic belief systems that attack people's faith, gender, race or other aspects of their lives. From unconsciousness comes a lack of respect and love for others. In this poem, Neverland is a place of unconsciousness.

The land of never-ending dreams is a peaceful place or heaven. Here there is no self-destruction. There is love and respect for our body, mind and spirit. As we learn to respect ourselves, we learn to respect others. Jesus' prayers can bring us back into alignment with our conscience.

When Jesus prays for us, he infuses life back into us. His fire of love and healing can bring us back to conscious awareness.

This poem could be helpful during difficult nights when we feel overwhelmed by life and cannot sleep. Let Jesus watch over your dreams.

Jesus Is Praying for Me Tonight

Mind and spirit drifted away
endless emotions
too much stress

But I will recover soon
Jesus holds my hand gently
He is concerned . . .

I fell asleep
went back to Neverland
the land of no one but the dead

Jesus prays for me
until I come out of my trance
puts me back into reality—his loving land

I am at peace
my heart is filled
with the sweetest light

He summons angels
to come by my side
to stay on guard and watch my back

Until I fully settle
in the land
of never-ending dreams

Jesus is watching
keeping my dreams

in case demons
try again their mischief

A goodnight watcher, Jesus
I feel calm and safe

Tonight I sleep well

Teach Me to Love

$\mathcal{T}$his poem is written in a plea-style form. It tries to describe aspects of the "life review" our spirits go through after we die.

During the major spiritual experience known as *dark night of the soul*, we experience a spiritual awakening or rebirth; we may witness collective judgement coming from souls in the spiritual world as well as from the souls of those still living in this physical realm. The dark night of the soul is a preview of our transition from this physical world into the spiritual one.

The aim of this poem and explanatory text is to provide information and bring awareness to the areas of our lives that need attention now, before it's time to cross over to the spiritual world—before we die.

During this *dark night*, I experienced excruciating pain and suffering. I felt hopeless and powerless, which led to feelings of resentment and distrust leveled against those who had caused me harm through judgment and condemnation. I went through a life review.

By following God's guidance, I began the process of healing and learned to forgive. I understood that sooner or later we all need to move away from toxic feelings and into a state of spiritual health through forgiveness.

God is love and he fervently encourages us to forgive and pray for each other and not to condemn. Judgement and condemnation of others carries heavy consequences. Prayers and forgiveness end the cycle of violence, not only in this physical world but also in the spiritual realm.

At times it seemed impossible to forgive. I asked God to help me transform this pain into love. I know God is eternally loving and a master at his craft, so I asked him to teach me to love and forgive those who judged my soul, so I could develop more spiritual strength and freedom. Anyone can ask for God's help and it will be granted.

The last two stanzas describe the capacity of our spirit to elevate the level of spiritual vibration or intensity (energy). When we feel down or low in spirits, we can ask God in prayer to fill us with his light. The higher the energy—the fire within our souls—the closer we are to God, and the more loving, stronger and happier we become.

If you find yourself unable to forgive or understand the dark side of human nature, may this poem be of use to you. May this poem light up the tunnel you are going through right now.

Teach Me to Love

How can I love the unlovable?
How can I feel love when I learned to hate?
How can a heart radiate when it is not strong enough?
And yet you expect me to send prayers of love

Love may be strong, but the anger returns
Anger remembers suffering even though it was taught to love
The memories of the soul feel the intensity of the pain
With pain, anger forms and it is hard for my spirit to grow

Teach me to love, dear heavenly father :)
For you love all and know not to forego
The lives of those in anguish
All you see is hope and more love

To reach the level of your existence
Seems too high. I seem unable to get
To the top of the mountain where the saintly live
Where all the feelings are pure ecstasy

To love those who caused pain
Is like caressing wood filled with spikes
To forgive proves a mammoth task

Only intense loving prayer
Can strengthen our quest
The higher the intensity, the easier to forget
The old pain and the bitter taste

Only you father can raise the vibe
Help us adjust to the new light
That enters our souls
Every time we ask

I See the Love

*T*his is a continuation of the previous poem, "Teach Me to Love." It invites us to see the good in people, to find their potential and accept each one. We all have faults and God accepts us.

One Play refers to a theatre play: one that takes place in a sky filled with stars—we are the stars in the play of life.

"If you dare to see it" inspires us to find beauty amidst the chaos of this world, invites us to see beyond what our physical eyes can see. The ability to see with our spiritual eyes is a gift we all have, but one that needs to be developed with God's help.

Life is like a poem (Poesía), and in it the characters (us) present different qualities and traits: some are aligned with principles of love and some are not.

The verses paint a scene—this poem represents your life; some verses paint a painful experience. After traumatic events, we can become bitter, rude, unsympathetic and distant. But there is always love within us and the possibility of change, and we can welcome the light back into our lives.

In this world, we all have the responsibility to take care of one another and find ways to uplift and encourage others. Love is our gift and it must be shared with others. Not sharing our love is considered selfish in the spiritual world.

Finding love in everyone by exercising our spiritual eyes helps us see deeply, beyond what our physical eyes can see. This can be laborious, but it helps us develop more tolerance and patience, which increases our capacity to love. The more we love the more we grow spiritually and the stronger we become.

I See the Love

I see the love in her
I see love everywhere

I see it in your face
I see it in your mess

I see the love inside
I see the love outside

I see it in the Light-ness
I see it in the Dark-ness

I see it in the Sun-light
I see it in the Night-time

I see it in the Sky
Early morning One Day

I see it in the dark
One Night, One Play

Love is everywhere
If you dare to see it

It is not always clear
You must read within

The lines of Poesía
The verses paint a scene

The vulgar words, obscene
The love hidden within

See the love in all
There is good in everyone

Perhaps not too much in some
But, all the same, a good start

Love Is Unconditional and Free

*T*here are circumstances in life when we have the opportunity to practice unconditional love by lending a helping hand, listening with an open heart, offering a hug, support, hope and peacefulness.

The title of this poem and the second stanza might seem contradictory: "Love Is Unconditional and Free" and "Love is to be given / not to be taken / without the intention of returning / love to the original sender." Loving unconditionally is a quality that requires exercise—like a muscle that needs to be exercised in order to get strong. To give love unconditionally is a practice that needs to be learned and nurtured. Love is not to be taken without showing gratitude by returning the courtesy. This principle is known as the law of reciprocity.

"It's best to leave a bird free . . . " There are two ways to read this stanza. In the first reading God leaves the birds free in the same way as he gives people free will. If we listen to God's calling and attend to those in dire need of help, then we know how to love unconditionally. Those who don't respond to God/Life's calling or the voice of their conscience haven't yet learned how to truly love. In the second reading the birds represent the people who walk away from us. Children, when they are old enough, walk away from parents; long-term friendships or relationships can disintegrate because of possessiveness. All people are free to choose. Life calls us to love others without possessing them, whether they are strangers or friends or family members.

Learning to love unconditionally is a process and takes time. Use the power of prayer to help those experiencing pride, arrogance and fear grow spiritually and open themselves to God's spirit and love. God loves you unconditionally and his love is enough to fill your spirit with joy, love, acceptance, patience and strength.

Love Is Unconditional and Free

How can I love you with conditions
When love is unconditional and free?
Give in the spur of a moment
When the feeling has just set

Love is to be given
Not to be taken
Without the intention of returning
It to the original sender

Love is abundant
Has so much vibe
Love is eternal and everlasting
Filled with magic and spark

Love is yours
Love is mine
Come and get it
Come quickly

Love is giving to the poor
Love is giving time and effort
Love does not overlook . . .
It longs to sing, it wants to heal

Give, not take
Wait! no regrets
For those who give, live
And those who take, don't

It's best to leave a bird free
Caging it is a pitiful deed
For those who are freed return
And to those who don't, you never loved

Jesus Is My Companion Tonight

*I*n this dialogue poem, Jesus shares his wisdom and knowledge. At times we don't seem to be getting the love, understanding, and support we long for from others. Some blocks to our ability to receive support and love are: the fear of being loved and accepted, a reluctance to ask for help, and also pride, which can limit our connection with others and stall our spiritual growth. If we don't remove these blockages, life passes us by and we miss opportunities for love and connection.

The world goes through suffering and chaos. Across the globe at any given moment of the night or day traumatic events are happening. All people experience painful and/or traumatic situations in life. Sometimes, the pain we experience may be misinterpreted as punishment from God. We erroneously see God as the abuser or as the one who does not stop acts of violence. Spiritual laws cannot be broken. There are consequences for behavior that causes harm to ourselves and others. Whether or not we experience consequences in this physical world, our spirits will be held accountable in the spiritual realm. God is always with us and won't allow us to suffer more than we can handle in this life or the afterlife. He is a healer and the source of love.

The pain each of us endures during difficult times can be a teacher. When we allow ourselves to truly feel the pain within ourselves, we can increase our level of compassion for ourselves and for others; through compassion we can learn to empathize; we can feel as others feel; we can understand and relate to their suffering—this is spiritual growth. When we resist feeling the pain and instead bury it deep in our minds and hearts, we are not giving pain the chance to transform us, and we stall our growth.

In this poem, Jesus gives us an important message: fight for the courage to light the fire of faith; find constructive thinking within yourself; take concrete action in life and move forward.

The "do or die" motto in this poem has a very special meaning: take immediate action to get through what is trying to block your progress. A spiritual connotation may be "do or wilt." To "die" here is to experience spiritual death. When we fail to act to overcome challenges, our spirits start to decay rather than bloom, and the fire within us diminishes. Also, giving energy to the negative only feeds it.

The poem ends with a key message: focus in an affirming way on how you see yourself; see yourself as you wish to be in the future: healed, stronger, healthier. Hold to the light!

Jesus Is My Companion Tonight

As I was pondering the vicissitudes of life
in came dear Jesus and sat next to me.
He asked me of my life, he asked me of my sorrows.

I told him my wants were unmet,
and my sorrows had taught me nothing.

Perhaps your ears aren't in tune, he replied.
Perhaps your heart is silent and deaf.
Perhaps your eyes want to see, but are halfway open.
Everything you need is passing you by—

How is that? I asked,
intrigued by His words.

Simple, but it may seem complicated, he said.
The hardest of lessons come with pain,
avoided by many and you tamb"en.
Avoiding your catalyst for change creates stagnancy,
and with this, life becomes a barren soil.

Pain is not to be confused with abuse,
is not to be seen as punishment,
is only what comes naturally—
on the path of life, "growing pains,"
if you choose to meet and overcome them,
are ushers to your future self.
Pain is part of your growth.

The more you learn to manage pain, the more you'll succeed,
but if you keep on avoiding it, how are you to rise to the challenge?
How are you going to fight pain without daring to do so?
It is the illusion that overcoming fear is complicated
that keeps you bound

Challenge the status quo:
fight and persist, for you can change what's done;
deeds don't stay when people stop feeding
the darkness which needs nourishment to survive and breed—
Only your fire can destroy it at once,
now and for always, if you so stand!
Courage means to act:
"Do or die" has survived through the years.
Best to die trying than to live hidden and shackled
to those who feed off your negative light.

Go out and enjoy all,
you so deserve it!
Dry your tears and embrace life.

To get what you want,
focus on life,
never on the opposite,
for it could show up.

Searching for God When He Is silent

I'm looking for heavenly father.
"Talk to me, talk to me.
Show me the secrets of your realm
that not many want to see.

Open my spiritual eyes,
shut my physical ones.
I want to find the truth
sans the emotions and the pain.

Give me an idea,
a story to write
so I can help others out of their plight.
May you bless us all in your own good time.

Hello heavenly father
Come to my aid
I want to hear from you
So much today"

Speak to Me

Speak to me of truth
Speak to me in truth
Speak to me for truth
May truth be spoken

Let's talk . . .

Finding God

O ur spirits have been eternally used to love and to singing love songs to God. When we come to this world and don't feel connected with God or don't remember who he is, we fall into worship of things or people. There is no need to judge yourself or others, but if it feels like you are constantly falling into dependency, it is time to look for God.

While trying to find God, I found that every person has a bit of God's wisdom. We are all pieces of a jigsaw puzzle that, when put together, gives a clear understanding of ourselves and life. God is the ultimate and complete source of all wisdom. We only hold parts of it.

Love is a feeling so elusive it can escape your grasp; many people search for the true meaning of love (see "True Love Is Not Romantic"), but they don't seem to be able to define love or understand it deeply. When we seem about to understand what love is and put the principle into practice, the concept escapes our mind's grasp. Pain, anger, fear or selfishness can block us from understanding and also from experiencing true love.

When life shakes us to our core or we take on more challenges than we think we can handle, we feel empty. It can be very difficult to give or receive love when we are empty or when our hearts are too tender and vulnerable. Willingness to heal can help us strengthen our hearts, and as we grow stronger, we learn to trust again.

The only true source of love is God. When the world seems against you, or life has brought too many tragedies and you can't seem to find someone you can trust, take refuge in the one who cannot and will not leave your side, ever.

Finding God

I was looking for God in a human
... couldn't find him
I was looking for a human to be God
... he couldn't be ...

I was hoping to find Love in a human
so I could worship him
I found no one ...

I would look endlessly for infinite wisdom in a man
I couldn't find it

I would search day and night
for what I couldn't find

an eternal dream
an eternal love
an eternal promise
eternal wisdom

a love like no other
a sacrifice for my life
one who'd lay down his life for mine

I couldn't find it

I traced the bits of wisdom I'd find in people
the pieces of a jigsaw puzzle
put them together ... always incomplete
I longed to find that which might not exist

After a long search, I found

that love is not a dream

love is a reality

a feeling so elusive
it could escape your grasp

a feeling so strong
it could shake your core

a feeling so extreme
it could take your sanity

a feeling so deep
it could drown you

a feeling so high
it could uplift you

a feeling sometimes
hard to give, hard to take

a feeling filled with truth
that no tongue could deny

Love is not a dream
is the fire manifested in us

Love is real

I found the source
the giver of Love
the one that stays with me forever
the one that lays down his life for mine
in exchange for nothing but love itself
the one I can trust

the one God

I Am a Love Poem

I am Love, said God
I start to write this poem

I am a poem
do you agree?

Skeptical eye, arched eyebrow
I reply: Explain please . . .

I am a poem
a collection of verses

a world without an end
an entire universe

I love you
and all of you

my children, my life
my reason to exist

my essence contained
in your physical shape

I am a poem
with verses aplenty

rhyming, without rhyme
loving without end

I am the powerful source of riddles
and their matching answers

unending source of Love
and its joyful essence

unending source of support
my hands are wide open

unlimited rest . . .

Do you want to hear more?

Me: Ad infinitum

Transformation

This poem is by far one of the most challenging I have written. It is rich in metaphor. And, the poem itself is a metaphor for human life.

The highs and lows creating a song, refers to the highs and lows of life we each experience and can learn from.

Love and hate intermingle in this world, but they are not one. They occur together in order for us to experience transformation.

Love is eternal and unchanging, and yet in the context of human experience, which finds us seeking spiritual growth, love is ever-changing, growing and evolving. When we forgive rather than give in to hatred, we grow, and we learn to love. When we learn to love more, we evolve spiritually.

Hate is stagnant; there is nowhere to go if we rest in it. Only love can transform hate and create spiritual evolution (growth).

"The dream" refers to the ultimate goal of life: to grow spiritually and reach God's realm. Spiritual evolution means transforming the dark areas in our spirit into light: anger into peace; revenge into forgiveness; hate into love. Painful life experiences have the potential to make us more empathic and increase our level of compassion. We learn to deeply understand other people's pain, and stop causing harm to others.

Thunder and lightning storms and tempests are the trials of life that rise and subside.

All is well, is one of God's quintessential thoughts, communicated to us by spiritual writers across genres and time. The phrase gives us hope during challenging times and encourages us to understand that all will pass eventually, and all will be well.

And the boat arrives on the dry shore—this refers to the end of human life and our experiences on Earth. The sunny side is heaven—God's realm.

It lands peacefully . . . At the end of our human trials, our spirits have the capacity to prevail, strong and intact. Our spirits never get damaged and are ready to exist in peace; the craving to pursue a life of chaos is gone.

The longing for peace away from paradise—This line might appear contra-dictory, but it is not. There are stages of spiritual evolution (growth), from infancy to adolescence to adulthood to maturity. Teenagers assert their in-dependence by creating their own rules and setting off on their own paths even if that means contradicting their parents. At an "adolescent" stage of spiritual growth we believe we can find "peace" (a false peace) away from a "nagging" conscience (God), and so we set sail. Everything looks good on the horizon until the storms of life arrive. As spiritual adults, we discover the mirage of a false paradise away from paradise (that is, away from the true paradise of Heaven or God's realm). Sooner or later we mature spiritu-ally and all go back to God, into a state of peace and love.

For when we left the cradle—means when we leave heaven or a state of peace and love in order to go through the storms of life and learn lessons that these experiences bring us.

"What is not" means darkness: experiences filled with pain and suffering. After enduring challenges, we long to return home to "What is," which is the land governed by the laws of love, harmony, peace, wisdom—God's realm or heaven.

"It is finished" is another iconic phrase used by writers across the ages. God uses these words to communicate his message of completion to the world. The last words of Jesus before he died were: "It is finished."

In the last stanza of the poem, "the final aim" refers to the culmination of human experience, wherein we turn toward and enter the permanently sunny shore of God's realm—a place of love, compassion, harmony, and peace.

Transformation

Life is ever-changing,
experiences are plenty, everywhere we go:
a beautiful rhythm of notes intertwine,
the highs, the lows creating a song.

God's love inspires greatness:
Greatness is the size of "the dream."
The price to pay is little for a dream so grand.
Rewards outweigh sweat spent
when in the end, success comes.

Love is ever-changing.
Hate is stagnant:
each clasps the other.
Love wins in the end.

No amount of pain proves
the power of love wrong.
In the end it's not love that will be gone.

As much as darkness believes it is real
and eternal, it is deluded.
Love proves darkness false.
Nothing lasts forever except love.

Your spirit is like a boat sailing
through thunder and lightning,
and as tempests rise and subside, onward spirit sails.
It endures the course of this outrage.

Brief, but seemingly eternal,
storms end, and . . . All is well.
The bitterness of the past is left behind
and the boat arrives on the dry shore.

The boat lands peacefully on the sunny side,
scratched but intact, and ready
for that longing which caused it to depart:
the longing to find "peace" away from paradise.

Sunshine projects the dream of calm,
but you learn that the dream will not last.

For when you left the cradle
and your adventures began,
you expected to have fun,
but instead you learned lessons.
You had far to go.

The boat is home,
the sailing's done,
the journey is over,
you experienced harm

and learned "what is not."

With harm comes pain;
no need to experience more of it.
It is now at an end.

It is finished.
It has been.
No more of that
is the final aim.

You want "what is."

Life is transformed—
Love wins in the end.

Who Am I?

A speck of joy
A speck of life
A speck of divinity
A ray of light

I am a speck of God's deLight

Don't Be Afraid, Just Believe

Are you afraid of falling asleep?
Will demons rob your peace?

Lie in my arms and rest
Don't be afraid, just believe

I'll get rid of your fears
While you sleep . . .

When you awake
You'll feel refreshed

Love

Love is strong
The glue that binds it all

It sparkles, shines
Love heals

Covers distances
That no human craft can cross

Love is warm
Love is all

Above all
Love is Love

God's Dream

*I*n the introductory stanza God starts creation—with his mind. He dreams a dream. It might be scary for our spirits to come to this earth and feel separated from God—which we never really are; we are always connected to God.

Our souls are in constant interaction with God, even when we are not aware of this. Before we come into this world, God sets up a plan for our lives. Each of us has a plan and a purpose. God reminds us when we have reached a certain age, and we agree to fulfill our life's plan. We partner with God to complete the purpose intended for our lives.

Our life stories are a series of acts. To act means to take action once you have found your purpose and path.

During challenging spiritual experiences, we develop the capacity to tap into what our purpose in life is; we wake up. The word *deLight* means from the Light or from God.

"A temporary idea" refers to the duration of our human life from birth to death.

The final test is a difficult one: once our physical lives end on this earth, we transition into the spiritual world. We must get rid of all our attachments to the material world; we must let go and embrace God's love.

God's Dream

God imagined a dream.
I was part of his dream,
a fiery flash that blasted off
from those fierce eyes.

Off I went into the world
Afraid . . . who cares? it's done.
Sooner or later I will realize
why I came out of his eyes.

Years passed in confusion.
There lingers a memory of the past,
a past memory lingers,
my heart remembers . . .

that I was born to play a role
on this stage called world,
God the director,
my helpers the crew.

All I need now is to wake up and
find my story and act and act!
but am I dreaming or am I real?
Finally, I remember . . .

that while I was in the storm,
God's hand stroked my turgid soul.
I realize the dream of his is mine.
I'm awake from a lengthy trance.

At last I see myself alive
within the chaos of this brutal life,
I remember who I really am . . .
a speck of God's deLight.

I realize
that I am the dream,
a figment of God's imagination,
a cosmic traveler,

a temporary idea,
a story with an ending.
After the adventures of life
back I go to my final test:

to leave this world behind
and embrace that Source we call Light.
Love is all I take.
I have finally left my mark on this Earth.

A legacy for others
to take
or to pass . . .

I see the Light . . .

How to Get to Love

This is a fun description of how our spirits travel back home, to God. Patience can be visualized as a robe of light covering our spirit. The rags of this world refers to all that is physical. The richer realm is the spiritual one.

The word "rags" is in no way an attempt to belittle our world. Rags symbolize everything that ends: houses, vacations, cars, pleasures of all sorts, and our physical bodies. They all come to an end after a period of use—they all get worn down. A richer realm symbolizes an eternal place.

My heart beeps, adds an element of connection between God's spirit and our spirits. We have God's spirit within us. What we feel, God feels. To illustrate this connection, visualize a remote control that turns on the TV by a click on the keypad. Similarly, when our heart beeps with love it connects with God's heart and this activates heaven's doors.

How to Get to Love

I transcend this realm "to" Love
using Wisdom as my rocket
and Patience as my robe

My heart beeps
announcing *its* arrival
far away the gates of Heaven part

My father is ready to welcome his beloved
I am so excited . . . joy starts
in my spirit, peace begins to reign

I am transcending the rags of this world
into a richer *Realm*
where no one has to bear

the hurt, the sorrow and the pain
I am traveling to my destination
in the vehicle my father has prepared:

Wisdom is my rocket
Patience, my new clothes
Joy comes gently, as I get close to Love

the final destination
God's final rest

His Spirit is so vast

there is plenty in Him to share
with all of those who long
to be in this blessed, blessed place

The Final Scene

*A*n age-old question: what happens after we die?

This poem imagines the last scene—when life on earth is complete. This vision came to me one afternoon and I quickly wrote down what was happening. The poem is meant to bring you peace—and knowledge that our spirit's final destination is God's bosom, the realm of pure love.

We are never alone, neither on this earth nor in the spiritual world. When our spirits commence the journey back to the spiritual world, we are greeted by angels, loved ones, friends we met on this earth, who act as our guides. They will show us the way home to God.

I was Light on that dream—"I" is each of us floating and dream is our vehicle. The angelic guide (in the shape of a man) represents those designated by God to greet us and lead the way to heaven. Every spirit in heaven is always filled with God's divine joy.

The people we meet in life are our teachers and also our students. A sister can be a teacher to her siblings and vice versa. A mother can be a student of her children and vice versa. Age does not dictate the role—a 5-year-old can be a teacher to a 60-year-old person. God gives wisdom to us all and all we need do is tune in to God's light present in each one of us, regardless of biological age. We are one another's guides. There are lessons we come to learn on this earth; for each lesson learnt, we achieve spiritual growth; the more we grow, the closer we are to God's love and compassion and the more we see him as our father, friend and partner in life.

No earthly feelings came by his side / neither did I feel earthly plight // We both are clear of worldly matters—This means once our spirits depart from this world, we go through a process where our earthly feelings are shed naturally, leaving us in the essence of our spirits: pure loving light. We feel lighter and embrace divine joy. On earth we love and care more for our family members and friends than for people we don't know—we are human. Once in the spiritual realm, our spirits align with God's spirit and we learn to love any person on earth equally and without preference. We experience "True Love."

After lessons are learnt in the time we are given on earth and we have fulfilled the purpose God has given to each one of us, we have achieved spiritual growth and our souls are ready to depart this earth and go back home, where God is.

The Final Scene

I was Light on that dream
I was light on my feet
floating toward that ethereal mass
that had the shape of a man

In the middle of the forest
He was waiting near a portal:
the entrance to a heaven with a Paradise
or a place of eternal peace?

A fest of greens and sunbeams
pervading everywhere
Dazzling, light-clothed
Imposing, towering pines

He was leaning on a fence
his arms crossed, one hundred yards away
the rays falling gently
upon his dirty blond hair

The peaceful bliss I felt
as I approached the chosen guide
An angelic one he was
not a prince of this land

He was standing there in such delight
his joyful semblance, his smile . . . divine
No earthly feelings came by his side
neither did I feel earthly plight

We both are clear of worldly matters
The final scene is being played
the final meeting before we enter
that mysterious portal, behind the veil

We both sense a feeling of accomplishment
something is finished, a destiny reached
With his help and my pain we both achieved
the final goal that God decreed

Once I reach his side
he will lead the way
into that magical place under the sun
filled with an eternity of celestial light

Goodnight and Thank You

Thank you for tomorrow
Thank you for today
Thank you for always
Always being there

Good night

Bibliography

Abbott, Rebecca. "Prayer Saved Thousands in Mallacoota." *Eternity News*, January 7, 2020. https://www.eternitynews.com.au/australia/prayer-saved-thousands-in-mallacoota-claims-atheist/.

"Australia Fires: Heavy Rain Extinguishes Third of Blazes in NSW." *BBC News*, February 7, 2020. https://www.bbc.com/news/world-australia-51409551.

"Australian Muslims Offered Public Prayer for Rain Amid Bushfire Crisis." *Daily US Times*, January 5, 2020. https://www.dailyustimes.com/australian-muslims-offered-public-prayer-for-rain-amid-bushfire-crisis/?amp.

Gladwin, Anna. "Rain Brings Relief to Fire-Ravaged Australia as Circle of Prayer Held at Glastonbury Tor." *Somerset Live News*, January 7, 2020. https://www.somersetlive.co.uk/news/somerset-news/rain-brings-relief-fire-ravaged-3711155.

Kramarik, Akiane. "Lifeline Miracle Network 2005." *YouTube*, January 8, 2014. https://www.youtube.com/watch?v=AZFbcf4JvSg.

O'Kane, Caitlin. "Police Officers Kneel in Solidarity with Protesters in Several U.S. Cities." *CBS News*, June 1, 2020. https://www.cbsnews.com/news/protesters-police-kneel-solidarity-george-floyd/.

19502163R00070